SILENT NIGHT, LONELY NIGHT

Random House, New York

Silent Night, Lonely Night

A new play by
Robert Anderson

FIRST PRINTING

Photographs by courtesy of Friedman-Abeles

Library of Congress Catalog Card Number: 60-10263

Manufactured in the United States of America
by The Haddon Craftsmen, Inc.

SILENT NIGHT, LONELY NIGHT *was first presented by The Playwrights' Company at the Morosco Theatre, New York City, on December 3, 1959, with the following cast:*

(IN ORDER OF APPEARANCE)

KATHERINE	Barbara Bel Geddes
MAE	Eda Heinemann
JOHN	Henry Fonda
JANET	Lois Nettleton
PHILIP	Bill Berger
JERRY	Peter De Visé

Directed by Peter Glenville

Production designed and lighted by Jo Mielziner

Costumes by Theoni V. Aldredge

SCENE

A room in a Colonial Inn in a New England town.

ACT ONE

SCENE 1. Christmas Eve.

SCENE 2. Later that evening.

ACT TWO

SCENE 1. Later that night.

SCENE 2. Christmas morning.

ACT ONE

SCENE ONE

A bedroom in an old colonial inn in a New England town.

It is a warm and comfortable room, full of atmosphere and mood. A fireplace is downstage right. Upstage there is the entrance from the hall, and in the center of the back wall a door to an adjoining room, which is locked. A window and the door to bathroom in stage left wall.

The time is Christmas Eve, the present.

KATHERINE JOHNSON *is an attractive well-dressed woman in her mid-thirties. There is much of the girl in her; a certain trusting innocence that is easily bewildered. She is sitting on the floor in front of the fireplace, playing solitaire. She is also smoking, and a whisky and water is on the floor beside her. She is not concentrating on the cards, or the smoking, or the drinking. They are mechanical actions. She comes to the end of the deck, and takes a puff on the cigarette and a drink of whisky, and doesn't go back to the cards. She just sits looking into the fire and beyond it into her own troubled thoughts.*

A town clock chimes the hour: seven o'clock. She puts out the cigarette in an ash tray and picks the ash tray up along with her drink and sets both on bureau. For a moment she fingers and looks at a letter which is lying open there—it is obviously what is bothering her. Then she tosses it down again as though she were not going to let it bother her. She picks up a pack of cigarettes lying among some things which have been fished out of her purse earlier, but then puts down the cigarettes, picks up the drink and fluffs up a couple of ribbons on

3

two Christmas presents which are lying on the bureau. Then goes to the window and looks out. There is nothing there to interest her. She makes up her mind to do something, and goes to the telephone.

KATHERINE   Uh . . . Yes. Could you tell me, if there's a movie house in the village? . . . Could you . . . I see, around eight. Thank you . . . No, I don't care what's playing . . . but, I see, thank you. Can I walk from here? . . . Fine, thank you.
> (*She hangs up. The door from the hall opens and* MAE *wheels in a room-service table with dinner for one set up and a small vase with a sprig of holly in it.* MAE *is a perfectly matter-of-fact woman in her fifties, who does her job well, rarely looks at anyone when she talks to him, and keeps busy straightening the room, poking the fire, emptying ash trays and generally tidying up*)

MAE   Sorry to be so long . . . We're a little short-handed in the kitchen tonight.

KATHERINE   That's all right.

MAE   The regular guests have gone home for Christmas . . . so they let some of the help have Christmas Eve off.

KATHERINE   Of course.

MAE   I suppose the manager figures everyone's got a home is in it.

KATHERINE   Yes.

MAE   (*Uncovering dishes*)   I think that's everything . . . Soup, roast beef, no gravy, salad . . . Shall I bring coffee later?

KATHERINE   No, thanks. This will be fine. I'm sorry to be keeping you.

MAE   I haven't anyplace to go.

4

KATHERINE   Oh.

MAE *(Indicating the studio couch)*   When you want the bed made up, let me know.

KATHERINE   I can manage that, thank you.

MAE *(Touching the holly)*   This was the cook's idea ... Holly for you and the gentleman next door and mistletoe for the newlyweds on the top floor.

KATHERINE   Oh, do we have newlyweds?

MAE   Yes. Strange place for a honeymoon. But then I don't know. Maybe it isn't.

KATHERINE   If they like it ...

MAE   They've been complaining of the cold ever since they arrived. Got two electric heaters in their room right now.

KATHERINE   It's too bad they can't have this room with the fire. It's rather wasted on me.

MAE   They probably aren't conscious what room they're in. *(She pokes the fire)* There's a double feature at the movie, if that interests you. Starts at eight fifteen.

KATHERINE   Yes, I've checked. Thank you.

MAE   The gentleman next door says it's very entertaining. He's been twice.

KATHERINE   Really?

MAE   The bill changes tomorrow. He says that's a good one too. He's seen it where he lives, but he says he's planning to go again. Poor man. His wife's in the hospital up on the hill. It's so sad. Afternoon show usually starts at two. I imagine Christmas won't make any difference. It's just another Tuesday as far as they're concerned.

KATHERINE Thank you for all the information.

MAE (*Adjusting the window shade and straightening the curtain*) That's the only important information in the town . . . What time the movies begin and what time the trains leave for Boston. Excuse me for going on like this, living alone I chatter a lot when I'm let loose.

KATHERINE I've enjoyed it. . . . Won't you stay?

MAE You mean . . .

KATHERINE Yes . . . While I eat my dinner. I'd be grateful if you would.

MAE No, I couldn't do that. Thank you all the same. I'm covering for most of the married help, and though I'd like to, I . . . well . . . (*She switches on the bedside radio*) There should be Christmas carols on this somewhere. It seems to me there's been nothing but Christmas carols since Thanksgiving. (*She gets "O Little Town of Bethlehem"*) There . . . (*She surveys her handiwork*) I guess this is what they call a home away from home.

KATHERINE Thank you.

MAE (*Going*) Anything you want, please call . . . I'll count it a favor if you keep me busy tonight.

KATHERINE Thank you. (MAE *exits.* KATHERINE *moves over to look at the dinner for one. She looks at it with a dread. The Christmas carols get on her nerves, and she moves quickly to the radio and turns it off. She picks up her cigarettes and moves back to the table and sits down, opening her napkin and spreading it on her lap. She tries to eat a spoonful of soup, but it is tasteless in her mouth. She picks up a cracker and nibbles the edge of it, but she can't continue. She tries to fight the terrible loneliness welling up in her. She is a*

6

girl used to controlling her emotions and she'll do it this time too. But suddenly she can't. She buries her head in her hands, elbows on the table, and suddenly she gives a half-involuntary strangled cry) Help! *(She is shocked at herself, and claps her hand over her mouth. Her eyes open wide to see if anyone heard. For a moment, there is nothing. Then there is a tentative knock at the door. She sits, frightened)*

JOHN *(Outside)* Hello? *(She doesn't know what to do. She is alert, waiting. Again a knock, a little louder)* Hello? *(KATHERINE rises and goes into the bathroom, half-closing the door behind her. JOHN knocks again and half-opens the door)* I'm sorry, but I thought I heard . . . *(He hears the water start to run in the bathroom. He enters, leaving the door open. He is a man in his early forties. He goes nearer the bathroom door)* Did you call for help?

KATHERINE *(Offstage. The water is turned off for a moment)* Everything is all right, thank you. *(The water is turned on again. JOHN is not quite satisfied with her answer. He looks around for a moment at the unfinished game of solitaire, the uneaten dinner. He sees the purse and its contents spilled out on the bureau, pokes his finger around the contents, and finds the bottle of pills. He looks at the key chain with its odd pendant. He goes to the hall door and closes it, staying on the inside. When KATHERINE hears the door close, she comes from the bathroom, dabbing her eyes. She is surprised to find him still there)* Oh . . .

JOHN I'm sorry. I just wanted to make sure everything was all right.
   (There is obviously an immediate contact between these two people, arising from the occasion, their own moods, and the strangeness of the situation in which they meet

—a certain unguarded nakedness of feeling on her part, a natural instinct of protecting on his)

KATHERINE Thank you. (*She goes to the bureau for a clean handkerchief*)

JOHN I'm in the next room and . . .

KATHERINE Yes. Thank you. I'm sorry I disturbed you.

JOHN Is there something I can do?

KATHERINE No. But thank you.

JOHN (*Realizing that there must be something he can do if her embarrassment can be forgotten, he smiles*) I could never stand to see a woman cry.

KATHERINE It's very silly and a bore. I don't very often. (*She has taken out a cigarette. He lights it*) Oh, thank you.

KATHERINE It's very embarrassing.

JOHN (*Trying to lighten the situation*) It's a woman's prerogative.

KATHERINE Still very sloppy. Self-indulgent.

JOHN My name's John Sparrow. (KATHERINE *smiles as she hears the name*) Yes . . . It's always good for a smile.

KATHERINE I didn't mean to—

JOHN —No, I like it. It's a name that gives my friends endless opportunities to exercise their wit . . . You know, the fallen sparrow, et cetera. (KATHERINE *smiles, liking him. But then her smile dies, and she turns away to the ash tray.* JOHN *tries to keep her interested and amused*) I see you aren't doing any better with your dinner than I am. I was eating my dinner, or trying to . . .

8

KATHERINE   I just didn't seem to ... (*She finishes with a shrug and a gesture*)

JOHN   My mother, who lived alone a great deal of her life, used to say, the most important part of any meal is someone to eat it with. (KATHERINE *smiles reluctantly again, appreciative of this man's efforts*) My mother didn't mind ending sentences with prepositions. As a matter of fact, she rarely ended sentences at all. She was a chatterer. (KATHERINE *just smiles at him*) Is this your first meal here?

KATHERINE   Yes.

JOHN   The food's really very good. (*Touching the holly*) I see they tried to cheer up your tray too.

KATHERINE   Yes.

JOHN   Somehow I resent their forcing Christmas cheer down my throat. Don't you?

KATHERINE   I guess they're only trying to be kind.

JOHN   (*Looking at the food*)   That looks awfully good. I've always been a great one for eating off other people's plates.

KATHERINE   Your dinner must be getting cold.

JOHN   Yes. (*Suddenly and directly*) May I bring it in here?

KATHERINE   (*Flustered*)   I'm going out.

JOHN   Oh, I see.

KATHERINE   To the movies.

JOHN   Oh. So am I. Eight fifteen.

KATHERINE   But I understand you've seen the show twice already.

JOHN   How did you know?

9

KATHERINE   The maid. She said you recommended it.

JOHN   It put me to sleep twice . . . which is what I wanted it to do. I go to the movies a great deal.

KATHERINE   Yes, so do I lately.

JOHN   Back in college I used to go to three double features on Saturdays. It was sort of a drug just to get through Saturdays. That was before I met my wife, the girl who was to become my wife. (KATHERINE *hesitates a moment, wondering whether or not to mention the hospital.* JOHN *continues matter-of-factly*) She's dead.

KATHERINE (*Looks at him, surprised*)   Oh . . . I'm sorry.

JOHN (*Making nothing of it*)   Five years ago. Thank you. May I bring my dinner in?

KATHERINE (*Thinks for a moment. She has never done anything like this before—instinctive and impulsive—and she is afraid, but there is such directness in him that to refuse his suggestion would be rude*)   Yes. I'm sorry to be so . . . But . . .

JOHN   May I ask you your name?

KATHERINE   Katherine Johnson.

JOHN   Thank you. I'll be right back, Mrs. Johnson.

KATHERINE (*She realizes that he has noticed her wedding ring. She calls after him*)   Perhaps it would be better if we went to the dining room . . . (*But he has gone. She stands there not knowing quite what she's doing. Then she moves her tray, and puts up the other drop leaf of the table to make room for his tray*)

JOHN (*In a moment, he re-enters, carrying the tray expertly on his shoulder, and carrying a bottle of Scotch in his other hand*) I worked my way through school doing this. (*Sets the tray down on the space she's cleared*) Thanks . . . One day I spilled a chocolate sundae down the back of the wife of the headmaster . . . She was very decent and wore the dress in again the following week to show me I hadn't hurt it.

KATHERINE (*Helping him arrange things*) That was nice of her.

JOHN I hope you drink Scotch. I've been sitting in there staring at this bottle longingly, but not daring to open it alone . . . sooner or later I would have.

KATHERINE You're stronger than I was . . . I've had one.

JOHN Another?

KATHERINE Not just now, thanks.

JOHN (*Making himself one*) Some people think drinking alone is very decadent. I just think it's very dangerous . . . I heard you turn on the Christmas carols for a moment.

KATHERINE The maid turned them on. I turned them off.

JOHN I agree with you. They're murderous when you're lonely. (*He pauses a moment—then, simply*) I'm lonely. I'm assuming you are too. (*He smiles*)

KATHERINE (*Is about to say something, but then she just smiles. She is touched by this man. She drinks off a little water from her glass, and holds it out*) I will take a little, thank you.

JOHN (*Pours a little Scotch into the glass*) Well, what shall it be? . . . Absent friends? . . . Snow for Christmas? . . . Or just that we manage to struggle through the evening without becoming public or private nuisances?

KATHERINE (*She is suddenly sad, and turns away*)

JOHN (*Goes on quickly*) I'm sorry. Let's make it snow for Christmas . . . and an early dawn. (*He drinks, turns his attention away from her so she can recover without embarrassment*) The roast beef has been very good here for twenty-five years. I came to school here and my folks used to visit me once a year and bring me here to the Inn for a feed. (*He looks to see if she has recovered, but she has just barely, so he goes on*) Disgusting how children can eat. I had a nephew visiting me once . . . twenty years old. Ate a huge breakfast and then for a finish settled down with a Milky Way.

KATHERINE You came to school here?

JOHN Yes. About twenty five years ago. A quarter of a century. Ugly phrase isn't it? I'm forty and I have intimations of mortality. (KATHERINE *smiles at this as she sits down and starts to eat, listening to him*) It's a wonderful age, really. You're old enough to sense it's not going to last forever, yet young enough to do most of the things you could do at twenty . . . I think I have an appetite. For which, many thanks. (KATHERINE *starts to eat the soup*) Shall I have Mae warm that up for you?

KATHERINE No, it's fine. Thank you.

JOHN Here, let me move some of this stuff away. Nothing less appetizing than a jammed tray.
(*He jumps up, and moves things to another table*)

KATHERINE Please sit down.

JOHN It's my waiter's instinct.

KATHERINE Please.

JOHN (*Sits and eats a mouthful—then*) Shall we do without the holly . . . or . . . No, I think it's rather nice now. Only we can consolidate it. (*Puts the sprigs together, with difficulty*) Damned hard stuff to arrange, holly. I don't know if you're aware of that or not. There. (*He eats a mouthful and smiles at her. She manages something of a smile back*) Do you play a lot of solitaire?

KATHERINE (*Remembering the game set up by the fire*) Yes.

JOHN My wife loved solitaire . . . We used to play double solitaire. I noticed you had a move you hadn't made.

KATHERINE I just got tired of it . . . I didn't try to finish. (*They eat in silence for a moment*)

JOHN Sometimes we used to . . . (*Suddenly stops, looks up, listening, very serious*) Was that the phone? (*He listens for a moment, then rises quickly*) I mean the phone in my room. (*He moves toward the door to the adjoining room*) Did you hear the phone? (*He listens tensely for a moment, standing at the door*) No, I guess not. (*His mood has changed. He doesn't return to the table*) May I bum one of your cigarettes now?

KATHERINE Of course.

JOHN (*He picks up the pack from the dresser*) I noticed this strange gadget on your key chain. May I ask what it is?

KATHERINE It's the eye of God.

JOHN What?

KATHERINE In Europe in saloons and bars they used to have little porcelain plaques with an eye painted on it . . . it was called the eye of God. It was to remind people that the eye of God was on them.

13

JOHN Hm.

KATHERINE My father found this little one shaped like a charm and gave it to me when he gave me my first housekey.

JOHN That's slightly terrifying.

KATHERINE Yes.

JOHN I don't know as I approve of that. (*Holds it up*) Kind of like a neon light blinking, "No!" . . . "No!" . . . "No!"

KATHERINE I guess that's what he meant it to be.

JOHN (*Returns to the table*) I believe they should paste a big label on youth! "Perishable. Use at once!" . . . When I was a student here, my life seemed fenced around with "No's". . . . I have a friend who has a little child, and when the child reaches for something he might break or shouldn't have, the mother says, "No, Becky. That's a No-no." My youth seemed to be filled with "No-no's." I wonder if it's the same for the boys here now.

KATHERINE I have a son here now.

JOHN Oh?

KATHERINE Thirteen. Just beginning.

JOHN It sounds silly to say, it's hard to believe . . . But I've said it.

KATHERINE That's why I'm here. He's been sick in the Infirmary.

JOHN That's too bad.

KATHERINE Oh, he's all right now, but they won't let him out until tomorrow. Something about his temperature being down forty-eight hours before they'll discharge him.

JOHN I seem to remember that sort of thing.

KATHERINE I stayed with him until they sent me away . . . gave him one of his Christmas presents . . . A recorder . . . you know . . . (*She demonstrates*) He's quite a whiz at it.

JOHN And when he gets out tomorrow?

KATHERINE He goes to Boston and flies to London to join his father for the holidays. My husband's on a business trip there. He's an engineer.

JOHN You said, "He's going."

KATHERINE (*Flustered*) Yes . . . I'm going to put him on a plane in Boston . . . I . . . I can't go just now.

JOHN (*Notes that she is flustered and goes on*) They make quite a thing of Christmas abroad . . . Paris doesn't do so much, but Rome and London . . .

KATHERINE You've spent Christmas in many places.

JOHN Yes. I guess I have.

KATHERINE (*Gently prying*) Did your wife like traveling?

JOHN Uh . . . I was alone. It was since.

KATHERINE Oh.

JOHN (*Rising to change the subject, he indicates the Scotch*) Could I interest you in . . . ?

KATHERINE No, thank you. (JOHN *hesitates over his own glass now*) I don't suppose you have a son in the Infirmary too?

JOHN No.

KATHERINE Do you have children?

JOHN (*Behind her back, he hesitates a moment, then quickly*) We had a daughter. Yes. Born a few years after the war. She was killed in an accident.

KATHERINE I'm terribly sorry.

JOHN (*Too quickly and urgently*) No, please. Please don't be sorry. I don't . . . Don't be sorry. It was all quite awhile ago. (*Now he does pour himself a light drink. Nervously, he goes on, with some banter*) You know my family motto is *Dum spiro, spero.* Do you know Latin?

KATHERINE I did in college, but . . .

JOHN While I breathe I hope. While there's life, there's hope. Somehow my friends found out about this, and it became "Don't spearo Sparrow." (*He knows this isn't very funny and smiles*) They thought it terribly funny.

KATHERINE It *is* funny. It's also a nice motto. *Dum spiro, spero.* Is that it?

JOHN Yes. *Spiro,* I breathe . . . *Spero,* I hope,

KATHERINE (*Mulling it over*) Spero. (*Looks at him*) Sparrow. (*Smiles*) It's nice to have a name so close to Hope.

JOHN (*Still bantering*) It's greater than Charity, isn't it? Or is it? I can't quite remember. Hope in myself, Charity in others.

KATHERINE And Faith in what?

JOHN In the morning.

KATHERINE Yes. That's good. Faith in the morning.

JOHN You're from the West, aren't you? California?

KATHERINE How did you know?

JOHN Oh, it's a different race out there. Sun-touched gods and goddesses.

KATHERINE You're from . . . ?

JOHN Born in New York. Educated up here in New England. Lived here for quite a while with four years out for the war. I've wandered quite a bit.

KATHERINE What are you?

JOHN (*Smiling*) I wish I knew.

KATHERINE I mean, what do you do?

JOHN Ah. At cocktail parties I tell people I'm a writer. That shuts them up, because they've never heard of me, and it embarrasses people to talk to a writer they've never read.

KATHERINE You're a writer then?

JOHN I wanted to be a writer. But I had a family that didn't think it was quite right to say you wanted to be a writer, so I said I wanted to be a teacher, and you know the classic phrase, write on the side. The war interrupted it very nicely. I was a flier . . . Navy, in the Pacific. Came back and became a newspaper man whose specialty was aviation.

KATHERINE That's what you are now?

JOHN Yes, more or less free-lance.

KATHERINE And the writing?

JOHN I did my duty and wrote my book after the war. Everyone said it should have sold better. It didn't.

KATHERINE What was it called?

JOHN *The Comfort of Your Company.*

KATHERINE It sounds like something I'd like to read.

JOHN Why?

KATHERINE (*Flustered at what might have been a too revealing statement*) I don't know. I guess it's the kind of title I like.

JOHN So did I.

KATHERINE Kind of title you hardly have to read the book.

JOHN A lot of people agreed with you. They read the title and had had it.

KATHERINE Was it based on personal experience?

JOHN Thinly disguised to protect people living and dead. Are you from San Francisco?

KATHERINE Yes.

JOHN I thought so.

KATHERINE Why?

JOHN San Francisco women have . . . Oh, a style, yet also a womanliness that is fast disappearing . . .

KATHERINE Was the story set in San Francisco?

JOHN Yes. It might have been you.

KATHERINE I was married.

JOHN So was I. So was she.

KATHERINE Oh.

JOHN It was just before Christmas. We were shoving off the next day . . . and I'd sat in a phone booth in the St. Francis trying to reach my wife back East . . . to say good-bye. I waited about five hours to get through, and then she wasn't in. No reason why she should have been . . . she was out for the evening and no one knew where . . . So I started drinking with the fellows in the bar, and suddenly it came over me that I had to say good-bye to someone, some girl. It was a big thing. I was going off to war, and I wanted to say good-bye. Only girl I knew was a girl I'd been out with with another officer on my ship. She was married, had a baby, and her husband was in the Pacific . . . So I called her up, but she had to stay home and take care of the baby. So I bought everything I could find, flowers, champagne, something for the baby, and even a couple of books, because we'd talked about poetry . . . and I took one of those wild streetcars out to her place. We sat on the couch and she played records, Jerome Kern, and we drank and I looked at the pictures of her husband's ship. She hadn't seen him in over a year, and we were both lonesome and sick inside. I knew from the way she looked at me, we both wanted to help each other over a tough spot. And she asked me if I'd like to dance, but I knew I couldn't, because if I ever held her in my arms even in dancing . . . And after all, we were decent, and her husband was in the Pacific, and her baby in the next room. Anyway, I finally got up to go home, and I shook hands with her . . . wanting to hold her and feel her warmth and give and take whatever comfort we had for each other. But we didn't. We shook hands and I left, and went back to my ship. I sailed the next day and was away for two years.

KATHERINE   And that was the story too?

JOHN   No. In the story he stayed the night. I wrote it that way because I knew that's what I should have done. You see a writer gets a second chance. Not very satisfying, but still . . . In those days I felt if I ever slept with anyone else, I'd never be able to be with my wife again. (KATHERINE *looks at him at this, expecting him to go on. It is obviously an important point to her*) I'm sorry. The conversation got a little out of hand.

KATHERINE   It's all right.

JOHN   (*He gets up to get himself another of her cigarettes—changes his tone back to the bantering again*)   I'll get you

19

a carton in the morning. For your stocking. Do you open presents on Christmas Eve or Christmas Day in your family?

KATHERINE Christmas Day.

JOHN My wife's family opened them Christmas Eve, mine Christmas Day. So we compromised and did it Christmas Eve. (*Notices the artistically wrapped presents*) My wife wrapped packages beautifully.

MAE (*In the next room*) Mr. Sparrow? Are you there?

JOHN Did you order coffee?

KATHERINE No.

JOHN (*Starts towards the hall door*) Mae . . . (*Stops. To Katherine*) Perhaps it embarrasses you?

KATHERINE (*It is a new experience for her, but she has committed herself*) No.

JOHN (*At the door*) Mae, will you bring it in here, please? (MAE *comes in, taking no notice that they are together. She acts as though it were the most usual thing in the world.* JOHN *turns to* KATHERINE) Sure you won't change your mind?

KATHERINE No, but I would like this thermos filled with coffee for the morning.

MAE I'll take care of it. (*Looks at the fire on her way out*) If you need any more wood for the fire just ask for it.

JOHN *and* KATHERINE Yes, thank—(*They look at each other.* JOHN *smiles, embarrassed, realizing it's not his fire*)

KATHERINE I think there'll be enough, thanks.

JOHN Oh, Mae, I've invited the newlyweds for a drink later on, so would you see I have glasses and ice and soda.

MAE   Ice, soda . . . yes . . . Four glasses. (KATHERINE *registers on the "four"; so does* JOHN) They're out walking just now in the snow. (*She leaves*)

JOHN   The help keeps track of every move those poor people make.

KATHERINE (*Laughs*)   I know.

JOHN   Barbaric custom, honeymoons.

KATHERINE   Yes.

JOHN   Newlyweds do something to a place. They fill it with a sort of infectious sensuality.

KATHERINE (*Smiling*)   I understand they've been freezing to death.

JOHN (*Laughs*)   I met the groom in the bar on my way in.

KATHERINE   Alone?

JOHN   Yes. He was having a stiff whisky and was buried in his gun catalogue as though it were his only contact with a fast disappearing reality. (KATHERINE *laughs*) He grabbed hold of me as though he were the Ancient Mariner. It turns out we're fraternity brothers at the school here . . . fifteen years apart, but still . . . (*He gives himself the fraternal handshake*) I think he saw in me the terrible future, and I saw in him the lovely past. Anyway, when he said, "There's still nothing to do around this town at night," I stifled my sympathetic laughter and asked them up for a drink later on . . . if they still had nothing better to do. (KATHERINE *is laughing freely now. She looks at him.* JOHN *continues, seriously*) I'm glad you're laughing.

KATHERINE (*She stops laughing slowly, and smiles*)   Yes. Thank you.

JOHN (*Looks at his watch*) It takes ten minutes to walk to the movies.

KATHERINE Oh, yes.

JOHN You still want to go to the movies?

KATHERINE (*She realizes how pleasant it is just to sit and talk, but she thinks the movies are best*) Yes.

JOHN (*Going*) I'll just get my coat and tell the operator where I can be reached in case there's a call. (*He goes*)

KATHERINE (*This concern for a call puzzles her. She puts on her coat and has almost reached the door when her phone rings. She stops, looks at it, and then returns and picks up the phone*) Yes? . . . London? . . . Wait a minute. (*She is upset*) Just a minute . . . Tell them . . . tell London I can't accept the call . . . No . . . Tell them you can't reach me . . . Thank you . . . (*She hangs up the phone slowly*)

JOHN (*Having put on his coat, he sticks his head in through the hall door*) Coming?
(*There is a slight pause. Then—*)

KATHERINE Yes. (*She throws her scarf around her neck as she exits after him*)

Curtain

Scene Two

As the curtain rises, we see the room lit only with one light and the glow from the fire.

The dinner things have been replaced by the set-ups for the four drinks—an ice bucket, soda, and glasses.

There is talk offstage, as the four people approach the doors.

JOHN (Offstage) I hope everybody likes Scotch.

JANET *and* PHILIP Yes, that's fine . . . That'll be great.

KATHERINE (*Opening her door*) I'll just leave my coat in my room. Janet, do you want to—(*She snaps on another light*)

JOHN (*Has entered his own room. We hear him calling out*) Didn't I ask for ice and things for drinks?

KATHERINE (*Sees the ice and glasses*) Mae left the tray and things in here. I'll bring them in.
(JANET, *still in her overcoat, goes out of* JOHN's *room, goes through the hall and comes into* KATHERINE's *room through the main door. She is bright-eyed, twenty-one and assured*)

JANET Can I help?

KATHERINE No. But come in.

JANET This is a lovely room.

KATHERINE Yes. It's a shame you can't have it. When I leave tomorrow, why don't you take over?

JANET I'm afraid we couldn't swing it. Up under the eaves for us.

KATHERINE (*Running a comb through her hair*) Oh, make him splurge for your honeymoon. It's terribly important.

JANET Oh, he'd splurge. It's me. I want to save the money for something, oh, I don't know, anyway something permanent.

KATHERINE You'll find a honeymoon turns out to be quite permanent.

JANET Yes, I guess it is.

KATHERINE Would you let me make you a present of it for a few days? I assure you I can afford it.

JANET That's sweet of you. No. Philip's parents offered to stake us to a grand honeymoon, but we're making them buy us a hi-fi and oodles of records instead.

KATHERINE It's just that young people never seem to realize how important honeymoons are till they're over. I know I was full of bright ideas about not wasting the time or money, and . . . well . . .

JANET I agree with you, but it's not as though Philip and I hadn't . . . I mean . . . (*Embarrassed*) Well, you know.

KATHERINE (*Not sure she does*) Oh, yes. (*Takes the tray and starts toward the hall door. She indicates the bathroom*) Do you want to go in there or anything, before we . . .

JANET No, but can't we stay in here? This room is so much more pleasant.
(*We can hear* JOHN *unbolting one of the double doors that separate the rooms. He knocks*)

JANET Oh. Shall I?
(*She moves to open the adjoining door*)

24

KATHERINE Oh. Uh, of course.
(JOHN *enters with the bottle*)

JOHN May I leave the door open so I can hear the phone?

KATHERINE (*A little taken aback by this moving in. She sets the tray down*) Uh . . . yes. Of course.

JANET (*As* PHILIP *comes in*) You know, Phil, this would be a wonderful color scheme for the living room at the farm.
(KATHERINE *closes the hall door*)

JOHN (*Busying himself with the drinks*) Oh, have you a farm?

JANET Not yet. Just a four flight walk-up on West Tenth Street with a flowerpot on the ledge. But one day we're going to have a remodeled barn or something like that . . . not in any fancy district like Westport or Bucks County, but someplace simple.

KATHERINE Sounds wonderful. Fixing your first house is one of the great experiences.

PHILIP (*Taking a drink to* JANET) There's a little matter of money first.

KATHERINE Well, get good pieces slowly. You think you're just getting something temporary and you end up having it for life.
(*Each time* KATHERINE *says something,* JOHN *gets a little more information about her. And each time he says something, no matter how casual, it registers on her*)

JANET We're not so keen on good pieces as we are on keeping it simple. I'll take orange crates and a big house full of books and records and children.
(*She smiles*)

25

JOHN (*Giving a drink to* KATHERINE) That's charming.

JANET (*She studies the colors and furnishings as she goes on*) My mother and dad, and Philip's, live in a clutter of Things with a capital T. Accumulated junk. Possessions which they spend a fortune to house and keep clean. And they're always bickering about the high cost of living. Sorry, Philip. At least mine are.

PHILIP Yes, mine too. (*Puts his arm around her to soften the criticism*) But I'm afraid our fifty-year program is hardly of general interest.

KATHERINE I think it's wonderful. I'm very touched by it.

JANET I know. You think it won't work. Well, we'll make it work.

KATHERINE Of course you will. And I didn't mean that at all. I'd like to send you a wedding present. Some records maybe.

JOHN What's your line of work, Philip?

PHILIP Oh, I'm just finishing off business school, and then I have a job in New York.

JANET Philip's always embarrassed to mention it, and I tell him it's ridiculous. There can be sincere advertising men.

JOHN Of course.

JANET Just as long as we don't try to pretend that it's of earth-shaking importance. It's a means to an end. If Philip and I can live the kind of life we want on some slogan that he dreams up, what's wrong with that?

KATHERINE Nothing at all.

JANET My father has a friend who lived his entire life on the strength of one slogan he thought up. I've forgotten which one it is, but you all know it.

JOHN   When better cars are built . . . ?

JANET   No.

KATHERINE   It's smart to be thrifty?

JANET   No. Well, it doesn't matter. Philip is embarrassed because he wanted to be a concert pianist, but his father talked him out of it. But we're going to have a piano. His mother is giving us one, and it can always be a hobby for him.

PHILIP   Jan, honey . . . these things are important to us, but—

JOHN   —I hope these things are always important to everyone.
(He raises his glass to toast this idea)

KATHERINE   And I hope you never quite achieve them all.
(She raises her glass)

PHILIP   Really?

KATHERINE   Yes.
(She notices JOHN *is looking at her)*

JANET   Why?

KATHERINE   *(Shrugs)*   It's better that way.

JANET   I guess I have talked an awful lot. I'm sorry.

JOHN   Please. We're loving it.

JANET   You're not laughing at us?

KATHERINE   *(Moved by their bright innocence)*   No, of course we're not.

JANET   The trouble with me is I've always been terribly enthusiastic about anything I . . . *(She has started to look for a handkerchief in her pocket and now brings it out with a shower of confetti)* Oh, I'm sorry.
(She tries to pick up the confetti)

KATHERINE Please leave it.
  (*She looks at it almost fondly*)

JANET My brother got into my suitcase and filled it with confetti.

KATHERINE (*Helping* JANET *pour some into an ash tray*) You'll never get rid of it. It will show up years from now on some dismal winter afternoon when you're packing to go home to Mother.

JANET My brother's a poet, or he's trying to be a poet. Anyway, he's living in Greenwich Village. We expect to have a lot of wonderful evenings together.

JOHN I'm sure you will have.

KATHERINE Where were you married?

PHILIP Well, we wanted to have a quiet wedding up here. Past two years we've been up here on week-ends a lot . . . (*Checks himself, embarrassed*) I mean . . .

JANET (*To Katherine*) That's what I meant.

KATHERINE Oh, yes.

PHILIP What?

JANET Just something I'd said to Mrs. Johnson about why we weren't splurging on a honeymoon. I'm sorry I interrupted.
  (PHILIP *looks to* JOHN *for a clue.* JOHN *shrugs his ignorance*)

PHILIP (*Disconcerted, goes on*) Anyway, we wanted a quiet wedding up here, because this place means something to us, but Jan's family thought . . .

JANET It's true. It was my family's fault.

PHILIP Anyway, it turned out to be quite a hassle.

28

Barbara Bel Geddes, Henry Fonda, Lois Nettleton, and Bill Berger,
as KATHERINE, JOHN, JANET, and PHILIP

JANET Terrifying.

PHILIP Janet tried to pretend it wasn't happening by carry-ing on a rapid-fire conversation with one of her bridesmaids about the United Nations . . .

JANET How do you know? You were at the other end of the church.

PHILIP I was told. Besides it went on all during the wedding breakfast, only by then the subject had switched to foreign aid.

JANET (*To* KATHERINE) Well, did you manage to get a quiet wedding?

KATHERINE No.

JOHN I managed it. (*Smiles smugly*) Or I should say, we did.

JANET Oh . . . Yes, of course.

JOHN We had the perfect marriage. Early June . . . small New England town . . . little white church with the sun coming through . . . and just the two of us. That's something to have had.

KATHERINE It must have been lovely.

JOHN And a minister who said very simply that marriages are not made in Heaven.

PHILIP Did our minister say anything? I don't remember.

JANET Yes, lots. But I don't remember either.

PHILIP You told him how wonderful it was.

JANET Well what are you going to say? A man stands up there and talks for ten minutes . . .

PHILIP I think he said he'd send us a copy of it.

JANET Oh, well good. I guess. (*Gently needling him—obviously, they share a joke*) We didn't bring along *enough* to read. (PHILIP *laughs, and then frowns because the others won't understand*) I mean . . .

JOHN (*Smiling*) We all do it . . . We all bring along books on our honeymoons so that they won't be a complete waste of time. (*They all laugh, the young ones in embarrassment. To* KATHERINE) What did you take on your honeymoon?

KATHERINE *War and Peace*.

JOHN You must have had a long honeymoon.

KATHERINE I did. But I haven't read *War and Peace* yet.

JANET Well, for your information, we haven't cracked our books either.

JOHN Good . . . Will you have another drink?
 (JANET *and* PHILIP *look at each other*)

JANET Uh . . . I don't think so, thanks.

PHILIP We'd better be running along.

JANET I haven't finished all my thank you notes yet.

PHILIP Uh . . . yes . . . Besides it's way after eleven.

JANET (*Holding out a hand to say good night*) I apologize if I've been a bore.

KATHERINE I'm sorry you feel you need to apologize. We're jealous. At least I am. Merry Christmas.

JANET Merry Christmas, and thank you. I didn't find out anything about you except you're going tomorrow. (*To* JOHN) Are you going too?

JOHN   No. I'm staying.

JANET   (*Confused*)   Oh.
(*She looks from* KATHERINE *to* JOHN)

JOHN   Mrs. Johnson and I just met, at dinnertime.

JANET   Oh, then we're all strangers.

JOHN   Yes.

PHILIP   Good night. Merry Christmas. Thank you. Sorry we
didn't get a chance to talk about the fraternity.

JOHN   Maybe we'll meet again in the bar . . .

PHILIP   (*Puts a finger to his lips and coughs slightly*)   Uh . . .

JOHN   Oh, sorry. (*He gives the fraternity handshake*)   Good
night.

JANET   Please don't laugh at us when we go.

KATHERINE   We're much more likely to cry.

JANET   Why do people cry at weddings?

KATHERINE   Oh . . . someday you may know. I hope not.

JANET   I don't understand that.

KATHERINE   Good.

PHILIP   I had a coat.

JOHN   Oh, yes, you left it in my room.
(*He goes into his own room*)

PHILIP   (*As he follows* JOHN)   Sorry. I'm always the one who
says good night and then exits into the coat closet.
(*He goes into* JOHN's *room*)

JANET   (*At the hall door, leaving*)   Did I make a fool of
myself? Going on and on?

KATHERINE Of course not.

JANET It's just that you're the first people we've talked to in five days. (KATHERINE *kisses her on the cheek, and sees her out.* JANET *joins* PHILIP *in the hall*) Good night.

KATHERINE Good night.
(JANET *closes the hall door.* KATHERINE *picks up the solitaire cards. In a few moments,* JOHN *appears in the connecting door to his room, fully conscious of the situation. He pauses there a moment*)

JOHN Do you think they'll make it?

KATHERINE Who knows? Let's hope so.

JOHN I always speculate at weddings . . . Is she still in love with someone who wouldn't marry her? Who does he dream about? What happens now that it's no longer stolen week-ends, but guaranteed weeks, months and years? . . . What happens? (*He comes in*) I never saw a more militant bride.

KATHERINE Weren't you and your wife that way?

JOHN Oh, determined for the good life, yes. Not simplicity. She was not a simple girl. I was the one who always was trying to find one great simple guiding truth on the head of a pin.

KATHERINE Did you ever find it?

JOHN No. At the moment I'm a man who's done almost everything and knows nothing.

KATHERINE That's very sad.

JOHN I always thought, if I had just a little more experience I'd finally know it.

KATHERINE What?

32

JOHN I don't know. Whatever it is. Some certainty. But all I found was a rage of contradictions . . . a saddening but somehow beautiful complexity . . . You whistle beautifully.

KATHERINE What do you mean?

JOHN You've been whistling ever since we met those two coming out of the movies.

KATHERINE I have a feeling you've been whistling too.

JOHN Hell, we're a world of whistlers. (*Toasts*) To the whistling walking wounded.

KATHERINE There's comfort in that. *"The Comfort of Your Company."*

JOHN Thanks for remembering. (*Looks outside*) Well, we got what we wished for. It's snowing.

KATHERINE That's right. We wished for snow, didn't we?

JOHN Among other things.

KATHERINE (*Looking out the window with him*) Is that one of the school buildings up there, with all the lights on?

JOHN I think it's . . . a hospital.

KATHERINE (*Looks at him*) Oh.

JOHN (*Pulling the curtains*) Somehow now we've got the snow I don't want it. Do you mind?

KATHERINE No.
    (*There is an awkward moment between them*)

JOHN I'll just finish my drink.

KATHERINE What? Oh, yes.

33

JOHN (*He walks past the dresser and sees the bottle of pills still there*) Were you about to try suicide when you called for help?

KATHERINE I don't know what I was going to do. I just suddenly found myself crying for help.

JOHN I've had it right there so many times.
(*He touches his mouth*)

KATHERINE I've always bottled up. I couldn't believe it when I heard myself crying out like that.

JOHN I imagine if we could hear all the stifled cries for help in the world, it would be deafening . . . Help . . . Help . . . Help.

KATHERINE Somehow I always thought it cowardly to cry out. I'm ashamed of myself now.

JOHN (*After a moment of looking at each other*) Nietzsche said the thought of suicide got a lot of people through a lot of terrible nights . . . Have you ever actually tried it?

KATHERINE No, not really. I suppose, like most people, I've thought about it.

JOHN I never quite had the courage to gobble all those sleeping pills or pull a trigger or jump. I beachcombed for a year, after my wife . . . died, and I used to put it in the lap of Fate. I'd get fairly drunk and then I'd go in swimming in the surf at night. If Fate wanted me, she could have me. She didn't want me. She always threw me up on the beach with the seaweed.

KATHERINE Why did *you* want to commit suicide?

JOHN Oh, general feeling of worthlessness, I guess . . . I can't imagine you ever had that feeling.

KATHERINE You can't?

JOHN No. (*Waits for her to go on, but she doesn't*) In the movies tonight, the sad picture, you cried out of all proportion to—

KATHERINE —I know. I'm sorry.

JOHN I told you I couldn't stand to see a woman cry.

KATHERINE Yes.

JOHN And when I took your hand . . .

KATHERINE (*Not wanting to go on with it*) Please.
(*She has turned away. It will take more opening up on his own part before she will open up. He switches on the radio*)

JOHN I wonder if they're through with their carols yet. (*Gets soft dance music*) Mmmm. I don't know. Is that worse than the carols or better? (KATHERINE *smiles and shrugs*) Does that happen to be a song that brings up pleasant or unpleasant memories?

KATHERINE No.

JOHN Then it can stand. Somehow I feel nights like this should be in a vacuum, having no relation to past or future . . . (*Getting back to the subject*) I never cried for help . . . but for years I had the desperate impulse to reach out a lonely hand to touch someone. The night in San Francisco in the war, when I went back to my ship, I wanted to reach out and touch the head of the girl who sat in front of me on the bus. (*In remembering, he has reached out his hand. He takes it back*) I didn't.

KATHERINE (*After a long moment*) Maybe I'd better say something. It may sound ridiculous, but . . . Oh, no, it *is* ridiculous.

JOHN Say it.

KATHERINE No. (*He waits for her, not helping her out of her spot*) Oh, all right. I . . . I'm very lonely . . . and I'm quite miserable and all that . . . but it's only fair to tell you I'm not going to spend the night with you. (JOHN *smiles.* KATHERINE *is now swept up in confusion*) You see it *is* ridiculous. But I only thought it fair to tell you, so that you'd . . . well, know. Now I suppose I've spoiled everything, and you're going to think what kind of woman is this who goes around assuming that every man wants to . . . It's just that . . . I don't know.

JOHN It's very touching that you should feel that you had to say that.

KATHERINE (*Running on, having trapped herself into making revelations*) I've never been with anyone but my husband, and I . . . My God, why should that sound prudish? Why should I feel I have to apologize for that. It's just that . . .

JOHN Don't apologize.

KATHERINE I'm not apologizing. It's just that, in this day and age, I seem like an anachronism. What the kids call a . . . a square. Isn't that the word?

JOHN Yes, that's the word.

KATHERINE (*Suddenly defending herself violently*) Well, I'd rather be that than a whore. (*She realizes that her defense is out of all proportion and has no relation to anything that's been said. She turns away*) I'm sorry. (*She snaps off the radio*)

JOHN Who's made you feel embarrassed about it? Someone.

KATHERINE Yes, I suppose they have. My husband's away a great deal . . . sometimes months. In the beginning, I

36

stayed home, I mean I didn't go out to parties when he was away . . . Then I started to go to my friends' homes, and of course they'd be very considerate and have a man to pick me up, take me home . . . very often husbands of my friends who were away visiting parents, or just out of town. I got quite a view of a lot of marriages.

JOHN And you learned to make your little speech.

KATHERINE Yes. I was shocked at how glibly people talked about going to bed together. As though you could fall in love in an hour.

JOHN You think people go to bed together only because they're in love?

KATHERINE (*She looks at him for a moment*) You obviously don't think so.

JOHN There are a lot of other reasons besides love . . . Reassurance, courage, loneliness, comfort . . . for protection against the horrors of the night.

KATHERINE You've been with a lot of women.

JOHN Yes. Too many, if that doesn't sound ridiculous coming from a man.

KATHERINE You see, you do the same thing I do. You apologize for your feeling that there could be too many . . .

JOHN What I said sounded smug as I said it.

KATHERINE (*These are things she has never had a chance to talk about before, and they spill out . . .*) There was one man . . . no, there were two . . . but there was this one man. I knew him and his wife. They were both my friends . . . and then his wife got sick, and it was hopeless, and she was five or six months in the hospital . . . dying. And this man, he was younger than I was . . . I used to go to the hospital to see his wife, and when she'd fall asleep for the night, I'd go out for a drink with him, sometimes bring him home for a sandwich, listen to him talk about how much he loved his wife, and he did. Why are you smiling?

JOHN What did you do? . . . I know the answer, don't I? Because you said you'd only—

KATHERINE —I didn't. He didn't love me. (*Defensive again*) Any woman would have done. A prostitute. (JOHN *shakes his head "No"*) Why not?

JOHN (*Too strongly*) Because with a prostitute it's a kind of mockery, and it leaves you more lonely than ever.

KATHERINE (*Thinks over his protest*) You think I should have done it.

JOHN I have no right to think what anyone else should or should not do.

KATHERINE Well, I didn't. And I've hated myself ever since.

JOHN That's too bad. I mean, hating yourself.

KATHERINE But I believe there is a book, a book we live by, and if we don't live by it, then we should stop saying we do, and throw it away and start all over again.

JOHN You've tried to live by the book.

KATHERINE Yes. I'm not strong enough to make up my own rules as I go along. I wish I were. I sometimes wish to God I were.

JOHN Yeah. The Eleventh Commandment is a tough one to live by. (KATHERINE *looks at him inquiringly*) Don't Get Caught . . . Funny thing is, you go around being afraid someone else is going to catch you, and you end up catching yourself.

38

KATHERINE My mother . . . (*Stops herself*) Anyway, my father took me away from her when I was seven. I don't know if she's dead or alive. I think she's dead. They say I look like her.

(*Her fear is clear from this statement*)

JOHN And your father gave you the eye of God, which has always said "No."

KATHERINE Yes. It has always said "No." (*She smiles*) That was the other time . . . I started to write poetry some years after I was married. I had been class poet at college . . . it was the only talent I had . . . and the home wasn't enough any more . . . We'd promised to love, honor and succeed . . . and he'd succeeded . . . So I wrote poetry . . . which I could never have published, because it turned out to be too personal. But I did send it to a young poet whose work I admired, and we corresponded . . . and one day he came to San Francisco to give a reading of his poetry. And he wanted to meet me. We had drinks after the reading. I don't know what he expected to find. I don't know what I expected to find . . . He was staying overnight in a hotel, and my husband was away on one of his trips. My God, no one stays home any more, do they? . . . And it was quite obvious what was happening over the drinks. We were talking about verse forms, but we knew each other very intimately through our poetry . . . and we were falling in love . . . At which point I opened my purse to get a cigarette, and nestled in the bottom with the lipstick and aspirin and Kleenex . . . the eye of God looked up at me.

JOHN And said "No."

KATHERINE No. It was more specific that time. "Thou shalt not commit adultery."

JOHN And have you hated yourself ever since?

KATHERINE (*Smiles*) No, not hate. Regret, maybe. But my husband came home the next day and I made him cancel all his appointments and take me to lunch . . . And I wanted him to spend the afternoon with me after lunch, but he couldn't do that, so I went and had my hair done . . . I wonder if husbands realize when their wives suddenly show up at the office and ask to be taken to lunch . . . I wonder if they realize it's a cry for help, for protection.

JOHN I think you've been steering through the narrows and shoals with wonderful dexterity . . .

KATHERINE And I got halfway home.

JOHN What do you mean?

KATHERINE I didn't quite make it, but I did get halfway home. Now? (*She shakes her head*) Next time you ask me if I want a drink, I don't.

JOHN You're not high. You're just . . .

KATHERINE Like the militant bride, I haven't talked with anyone in five days, or five years . . . or ever, like this. Why did you stop me whistling?

JOHN Because of the way you held my hand in the movies.

KATHERINE (*Goes to her purse on the bureau*) I think I'd better take one of my unwinders.
(*She takes out a pill box and fishes for a pill*)

JOHN What's that?

KATHERINE I don't know exactly what they are, but they unwind me, get me ready for sleep . . . sometimes. If they don't, then I have others . . .

JOHN Yes, I saw those.

KATHERINE It's funny. Usually people unload on me. I'm sorry. I'm really sorry. You won't think so much of San Francisco ladies after this. Out there I'm famous for not even giving my name except at the point of a gun.

JOHN I'm flattered and touched that you'd talk to me like this.

KATHERINE I gather you've heard many astounding stories about marriage. I suppose most of them are the same.

JOHN (*He holds up his thumb*) Like thumbs, all alike. Like thumb prints, all different.

KATHERINE Who said that?

JOHN I'm afraid I did.

KATHERINE What are you doing here alone in a God-forsaken spot on Christmas Eve?

JOHN (*Thinks for a moment*) I'm evading the kindness of friends, and enjoying the kindness of a stranger.

KATHERINE I know what you mean.

JOHN I could have toddled along to friends' houses to help them trim the tree. But I decided not to this year.

KATHERINE I can understand.

JOHN Christmastime and Thanksgiving . . . it's an offense against something or other to be single. My wife and I used to gather in our friends who were alone. I never realized how lonely we were making them feel. It's much better to be with strangers . . . to make your own "family" as it were, for a few hours.

KATHERINE Yes.

JOHN I was in Paris one year at Christmas. And New Year's Eve in the subways, all the single men and women were headed for parties with their nicely wrapped bottles under their arms. Their tickets of admission.

KATHERINE   Where were you going?

JOHN   I don't remember where I was going. But I know where I ended up. Did you know the French don't sing "Auld Lang Syne"? I got very maudlin about old acquaintances, and the girl had never heard of it.
(*He starts to whistle it, then stops*)

KATHERINE   You manage to find compatible strangers wherever you are.
(*They look at each other a long moment. He is suddenly serious, a little hurt by this. He moves away*)

JOHN   That kind of woman is easy to find.

KATHERINE   A man as attractive as you, I should think—

JOHN   (*Bluntly, directly*)   I've made it a practice for two years not to sleep with anyone I could possibly care for.

KATHERINE   How terrible!

JOHN   There are more terrible things. (*He moves away*) I don't know why I told you that. I suppose it's because you told me you had no intention of sleeping with me. I just wanted to put your mind at rest. (*Goes to the bottle*) You sure you won't have some more?

KATHERINE   I seem to be suddenly sobered. All right.
(*He pours for her and gives her ice*)

JOHN   (*As he pours, he starts to smile*)   I'm sorry. That was uncalled for. Very ungentlemanly.

KATHERINE   I think I asked for it.

JOHN Seems impossible to think this is the same little gentleman who used to push his mother's chair to the table downstairs in the dining room.

KATHERINE I would like to have seen you then.

JOHN No you wouldn't have. I was a very proper little prig. Mortally afraid of anything even slightly off the straight and narrow, and hiding my fear behind a pompous self-righteousness. How could the seniors make love to the town girls down by the river on spring evenings . . . When all the time I was aching to do it myself. So much morality is just lack of opportunity, or lack of courage, or lack of appetite . . . Lest you draw the wrong conclusions, mine was lack of courage.

KATHERINE (*Smiles*) So I gathered from what you said earlier. (*The clock outside starts to strike twelve*) It's Christmas.

JOHN Yes. Officially. (*Draws the curtains aside a bit*) When I was a student here I used to lie awake at night listening to those bells. The simplicity of the half-awake dreams I used to make up for myself!

KATHERINE That someday you would find the answer on the head of a pin?

JOHN Oh, no. I knew the answer in those days. Do right, work hard. Be honest, and there'd be a big reward for you on Prize Day . . . Now I know there is no Prize Day. My wife was as near to being a saint as anyone could be on this earth, and there was no Prize Day for her. (*He has suddenly blurted this forth. He looks up, surprised, then smiles and holds up his glass*) But there are small comforts along the way. You said you'd gotten halfway home. What did you mean?

43

KATHERINE I changed the subject.

JOHN I'm changing it back again . . . if I may.

KATHERINE My father once told me that one should be very careful what one writes or says late at night. You are.

JOHN Yes, I am.

KATHERINE (*She sits at the desk, and draws the letter from the pigeonhole and just places it in front of her*) Two days ago, just before I left California, I got a letter from my husband. It's very touching, really . . . touching, and yet to me, terrifying. I mean, I know a husband can't be away as much as he is without something happening, but a woman always expects or hopes it's something meaningless . . . or she tries not to think about it at all . . . Some friends of mine came back from London and tattled.

JOHN I'm sorry.

KATHERINE He knew they would. So he wrote me this letter. (*She picks up the letter and reads a bit from it*) "It's a defenseless position, but I won't come crawling with this over my head for the rest of my life. And I can't blame you if you want a divorce. But I hope you won't. It happened, and, to be honest, it's happened before. I'm bewildered and feel terribly isolated. I have tried. I have seen hundreds of movies alone in all the languages of the world. I know I have put you in an impossible situation . . ."
   (*She almost breaks*)

JOHN He's very honest.

KATHERINE Yes. He's honest and honorable. I think sometimes that's why he married me. I was the first girl he'd . . . been with . . . and I think he never questioned that that meant marriage. Oh, that sounds dreadful. We were in love. In college I had a little apartment, and he made it his home. I think when senior year was over, we just didn't know what else to do. We were neither one of us very adventurous, and I guess we were both glad to find a safe harbor. We'd had a wonderful relationship, and we didn't want it to end. But it did end with marriage, in a sense, with the first bills and responsibilities. My friends who have seen her say she looks like me. Strange.

JOHN What are you going to do?

KATHERINE I don't know. (*She goes to the window*) It's a terrible decision to have to make.

JOHN That's why you're not going to London, then?

KATHERINE Yes . . . My husband called earlier this evening, but I wouldn't take the call. I need time.

JOHN You're thinking of leaving him then?

KATHERINE Yes. (*Turns to him, defensively*) I committed myself to the marriage. Do you know what that means?

JOHN Yes.

KATHERINE It wasn't a one-foot-in, one-foot-out, ready-to-jump sort of thing . . . as long as it's convenient, as long as it doesn't get in the way of my self-expression. I think I terrified him with my sense of dedication. I wanted to dedicate my life blindly. It frightened him. He wanted the more loosely knit relationship we'd had in college . . . I wanted to fulfill his life as he would fulfill mine . . . not just have a . . . a marriage of convenience . . . not just friends who slept together! . . . I sound so bitchy. But I'm hurt . . . You don't say anything.

JOHN I don't know anything to say.

45

KATHERINE Somehow it's all right until someone gives you the feeling you're being cheated . . . I had an aunt who thought she'd been happily married till she read an article about sex enjoyment. After that she thought she'd had a terrible marriage and got a divorce. Now she's alone someplace in an apartment hotel and spends her evenings walking her dog. (*They smile sadly at this*) Why do you sleep only with women you can't care for?

JOHN I've told my story too many times to too many people.

KATHERINE Were you happily married?

JOHN Yes.

KATHERINE Then why didn't you marry again?

JOHN (*Not wishing to go into this*) I could explain your husband to you.

KATHERINE No.

JOHN I'd like to.

KATHERINE Nobody needs to explain longing and desire to me. Were you faithful to your wife?

JOHN Yes.

KATHERINE You said there'd been no Prize Day for her. (JOHN *doesn't answer*) How long were you married?

JOHN Oh, 1940 . . . nineteen years.

KATHERINE But you said she'd been dead five years.

JOHN Did I? (*He looks at her a moment, then moves toward his door. She watches him, puzzled. He sees her sleeping pills on the desk*) May I have a couple of your sleeping pills? I forgot mine.

46

KATHERINE (*Going to the desk and giving him one*) Yes . . . One should do.

JOHN (*Looks at the pill in his hand*) Mine are pink . . . though I've had some luck with the yellow and white ones. Can't take the blue ones. Thank you. Good night.
(*He goes to his door*)

KATHERINE Good night.
(*She goes to her bed, thinking he has gone . . . and sits. JOHN stands in his doorway, watching her. He sees her bury her head in her hands. He is touched by this misery, and moves back into the room and sits and then lies on the couch. She turns around and watches him*)

JOHN I don't particularly want to be alone tonight. Do you mind? (KATHERINE *smiles and shakes her head "No."*) Christmas Eve is Hell, isn't it? (*She smiles at him*) The Fourth of July is much easier.
(KATHERINE *takes a blanket from the top of her bed, and comes over to the couch. She turns out the lights near the couch, and puts the blanket over him. As she pulls it up around his shoulders, he turns away. She looks at him, surprised, wondering. She crosses to her bed, and sits down and starts taking off her shoes, as*)

The Curtain Falls

ACT TWO

Scene One

As the curtain rises, the only light in the room is from the fireplace. JOHN *is asleep on the couch, restless and mumbling in his sleep.*

KATHERINE *is still in her sweater and skirt, and is lying on the bed with a blanket over her. She is propped up on one elbow, watching* JOHN *and listening to him. Then she lies back on the pillow.*

In the distance a town clock strikes five.

JOHN (*Suddenly he sits bolt upright and listens. He looks over at* KATHERINE, *but thinks she is asleep. His main attention is elsewhere. He throws off the blanket and jumps up and goes to his door and listens. He hears nothing, but he goes into his room, and we hear him at the phone*) Hello . . . I'm sorry to disturb you, but I'm expecting a call and I thought I heard the phone . . . You're sure . . . All right. Thank you. (*We hear him hanging up.* KATHERINE, *puzzled by this, sits up and looks toward his door. In a moment, he comes back in*) Sorry. I thought my phone was ringing. (*He walks over to light her cigarette*)

KATHERINE That's all right . . . Thanks. (JOHN *moves an ash tray to the edge of her bed*) Thanks.

JOHN Did you sleep at all?

KATHERINE A little.

JOHN Sorry to wake you up.

KATHERINE I was awake.

JOHN Oh.

KATHERINE I was listening to you moan in your sleep.

JOHN (*Shaking his head*) Oh . . . Just crack me one when I do that. Doctor told my wife it was no good waking me up by talking to me . . . Just slap me hard. Apparently that gets down to the subconscious where the moaning is going on. So next time crack me one.

KATHERINE (*Smiling*) Yes. I'll remember next time.

JOHN (*Smiles when he realizes how foolish it was to say "next time"*) That's right. Well . . . (KATHERINE *swings around and sits on the bed. He notices that she's still dressed*) I'm afraid I messed up your night for you. Kept you from getting properly to bed.

KATHERINE This is the way I wanted it.

JOHN Really?

KATHERINE It was nice to wake up and see you . . . to see somebody, sleeping there.

JOHN It's terrible.

KATHERINE What?

JOHN To be part of a woman's life again.

KATHERINE Terrible?

JOHN (*Smiles*) Yes. Quiet like this. Just sharing the room. Someone to talk to at night when you wake up . . . when you're frightened of the dark . . . Someone to get an ash tray for.

KATHERINE But there have been many women.

JOHN Yes. But they always got up and went home. Or I got up and went home . . . There's a certain mystical thing about spending the night . . . I've never spent a night like this before.

KATHERINE   Neither have I.

JOHN   (*Turns and looks through the curtains*)   It's stopped snowing . . .

"... the world, which seems
To lie before us like a land of dreams,
So various, so beautiful, so new,
Hath really neither joy, nor love, nor light,
Nor"—

What? I don't remember. I think I used to recite that to my first girl . . . and I wrote it in a letter to my wife during the war . . . My wife and I, we bought two copies of the same book of poems, *The Golden Treasury,* and we marked each one with a date . . . and while I was away, we were going to read the same poem at the same hour of the day.

KATHERINE   How nice.

JOHN   Of course it took quite a bit of planning, figuring out changes in time, and international date lines, et cetera . . . I was reading, "Shall I compare thee to a summer's day," when we were hit by a torpedo.

KATHERINE   Your wife sounds as though she had been very much a kindred spirit, as though you were very close.

JOHN   (*Smiles*)   She stopped me from going to three double features on Saturdays.

(*He picks up her cigarette from the ash tray and takes a puff*)

KATHERINE   (*Smiles*)   How old were you when you met her?

JOHN   A very innocent eighteen.

KATHERINE   My God!

53

JOHN Yes, my God! To really fall in love for the first time at eighteen, and suddenly to have your whole life fall into focus. It's a miracle, isn't it? That only happens once. You don't ask, Am I in love? Is this real? Will it last? It suddenly just pours over you like sunshine . . . and you breathe deeply as though for the first time. And you're wide open. You confess your sins, and she confesses hers. My God, what little sins . . . and you forgive each other and fall into each other's arms.

KATHERINE Did you really have it like that?

JOHN Yes, so help me God. It seemed to be four years of spring. She lived with her family in Boston, but they were always away, around the world, or abroad, and so we were like children playing house on Beacon Hill. I'd been a very mediocre student, and suddenly, nothing but A's. At first the college thought I was cheating . . . but I was only in love. And there seemed to be time for everything in those days. We sailed at Marblehead, we skied in New Hampshire, and we lay in each other's arms for hours and hours just filled with the wonder of it. All we could say was, "It's wonderful, isn't it?" . . . "It's marvelous, isn't it?" . . . "Aren't we lucky?" . . . Went to the theatre, up in the second balcony . . . once a month Sunday lunches at the Ritz and a walk up the Charles River, and then the long afternoon in front of the fire in her living room . . . Every summer I went to summer school to be near her. My parents marveled at my thirst for knowledge . . . But surely you had this too. All young lovers do.

KATHERINE No.

JOHN I can't believe it.

KATHERINE I believe you.

54

JOHN Sorry. I'm truly sorry.

KATHERINE Don't misunderstand. We had a wonderful time. But it wasn't like that. It wasn't his temperament, or perhaps mine.

JOHN I have letters we wrote each other. It didn't seem enough to see each other every day. We wrote letters too, and handed them to each other. It seemed silly at the time. I've grown grateful for that silliness. One should commit one's love to paper. Like photographs, love letters grow in importance . . . "Oh, did I look like that?" . . . "Did you look like that?" . . . Friends of mine had movies taken of their garden wedding. When they showed the film to their children fifteen years later, the oldest said, "My, Daddy loved Mommy then, didn't he?" One should commit one's love to paper. Though sometimes it's . . .
    (*A new thought darkens his mind, and he stops*)

KATHERINE Dangerous.

JOHN Yes.

KATHERINE —One day my husband came across my poems. It was like coming across the truth locked in a drawer. I had expressed my loneliness so directly, almost nakedly.

JOHN What did your husband say?

KATHERINE It's not what you think. I looked into a window from the garden, and saw he was reading them. He didn't see me. I went upstairs to our room, and waited. I lay down and stared out the window and waited. He came up in a while and looked at me. I could see he'd been crying. He lay down beside me and held me in his arms. It almost killed me. He didn't say anything. He just held me for a very long while. He never said anything about them.

JOHN The footsteps of doves.

KATHERINE What?

JOHN Someone said, "The great crises in our lives come not with the sound of thunder and lightning, but quietly like the footsteps of doves."

KATHERINE Yes.

JOHN Like sun suddenly breaking over you . . . or night.

KATHERINE For quite a while after that, we were very gentle towards each other. I, because I knew I had hurt him. He, because he realized now my loneliness in our relationship.

JOHN I always treated my wife so that people wouldn't know we were married. I think early in my life I was frightened by a middle-aged couple at a summer resort. They sat just opposite me in the dining room, and they never talked. I've seen couples in Paris and Rome, on that long-saved-for holiday together, staring at their plates, and wondering why they'd come. I often thought they should have swapped wives for the trip.

KATHERINE But you chattered.

JOHN Yes. Like a magpie. Or I'd just smile at her. Or I'd tease her. Anything to keep contact. I wanted to prove against all the evidence around me that it could work. On a rainy afternoon for no reason I'd send her some spring flowers . . . There were hundreds of anniversaries to remember. The day we met, the day we first kissed, the day we first slept together . . . the day we decided to get married. You know. Every couple has them.

KATHERINE You really worked at it, didn't you?

JOHN   I hate looking into a flower shop and seeing a lovely bunch of white lilacs or the first tulips, and not having anyone to send them to. I hate having nothing to give you.

KATHERINE   You've given me a great deal already. You've given me this night.

JOHN   No. I've taken that . . . from you.

KATHERINE   It's nice that we should both feel that way.

JOHN   Yes. (*They look at each other for a moment, then* JOHN *goes to the window and looks out*) We're almost through it without disturbance, public or private.

KATHERINE   Yes.

JOHN   (*Looking out the window*)   You know, when my wife first . . . first after my wife died, people were very kind and did everything for me . . . always asked what else they could do. I couldn't ask a woman what I really wanted . . . "Come home and be with me all night. Just let me hold you all night." . . . What I wanted was to hold someone.

KATHERINE   When I go visit my father, who's in his seventies, he always says, "Just hold me a little for a moment . . . Let me hold you."

JOHN   Yes. Hold me . . . Hold me . . . Help . . . Help.

KATHERINE   (*After looking at him a long moment*)   Your wife is not dead, is she?

JOHN   What?

KATHERINE   Your wife is not dead. She's in that hospital up there, isn't she?

JOHN   Yes. How did you know?

KATHERINE   The maid told me.

JOHN You've been very patient then.

KATHERINE Do you want to tell me about her? (*When she gets no answer, she goes on*) I feel you've been waiting . . . inviting questions and then shying away from them. Why do you say she's dead? Is it very serious? I mean your wife's illness.

JOHN Yes, serious but not fatal.

KATHERINE The phone call you keep expecting then is . . . ?

JOHN Yes.

KATHERINE But if it's not fatal?

JOHN (*With difficulty, but unemotionally*) My wife is . . . The hospital is a sanitarium . . . My wife is insane.

KATHERINE Oh, I see.

JOHN If I'd told you that earlier on, I would have found the evening intolerable.

KATHERINE Why?

JOHN Just the way you looked at me now.

KATHERINE How long has she been there?

JOHN Five years.

KATHERINE And what hope is there?

JOHN (*Ignoring this piecemeal questioning*) I told you we'd had a wonderful marriage. We did. A lovely daughter of five.

KATHERINE Oh, yes . . . the accident.

JOHN Yes, in a sense. The accident of my becoming infatuated with another woman after fourteen years of marriage.

Don't ask me why or how. I've spent five years trying to rationalize what I did. But I did. I became helplessly, shamefully infatuated. Nothing happened. She was married and didn't really care for me. I wrote her many letters, many, many letters. And one day, for the first time, she wrote me a letter . . . My wife for some reason opened it. The address looked like Mrs. instead of Mr. . . . I don't know. And quite naturally, quite humanly she read it . . . It was a letter telling me that I must not love her . . . this woman telling me . . . While she had been reading the letter, our child had wandered into the neighbor's property and had fallen into the pool and drowned . . . Four months later, we brought my wife up here . . . (KATHERINE *makes a move toward him of sympathy. Sensing the move, he turns deftly away*) I didn't think that was a story for a Christmas Eve. As a matter of fact, I don't any longer think it's a story for any time. It's much easier to say she died.

KATHERINE   It sounds silly to say, "I'm so sorry."

JOHN   Please don't say it. I'm sick of pity! . . . When it started happening to my wife, everyone was full of sympathy and pity. I wanted to tell them about the letter . . . to show them that I had driven her insane. But I couldn't . . . I wanted to kill the woman who had written the letter. I wanted to kill myself. And all the time there was pity. And I accepted their pity, and hated myself for needing it. How wonderfully ready women are to heal by the laying on of hands and lips. My God, how healing.

KATHERINE   So you have run away from comfort, from pity.

JOHN   At first I tried to visit my wife every day. But she didn't know who I was, and seemed to be worse when I saw her. The doctors suggested I stay away for a long while. I did. I left the country and started wandering . . . I looked for and found solace in sensation . . . I wanted to hit bottom. Have you ever had that feeling?

KATHERINE No.

JOHN (*Drily, but with self-contempt*) I became a scavenger. I scavenged off unhappy marriages. Having destroyed my own marriage, I wanted to prove that other marriages could be destroyed . . . Did you know it's ridiculously easy to be a lover? . . . Especially if you've been married. You know all the little sufferings that a wife endures, that you've made your own wife endure . . . I almost succeeded in making a mockery of everything, in reaching absolute zero . . . Then one morning in Lisbon I knew. I knew that this rock bottom I'd been trying to reach was not rock, was not something you'd spring back from alive and purged . . . It was muck and swallowed you up . . . And I came home.

KATHERINE Is there a chance your wife will get well?

JOHN No. But when the doctors all say "No," you begin to believe in mysteries, superstitions. You remember, "If I can walk home without stepping on a crack in the sidewalk . . ."

KATHERINE I remember.

JOHN I don't know why . . . perhaps because of the thing that started it, the letter, but I began to think that as long as I didn't love anyone else, or sleep with anyone I cared about, she would somehow know I loved her and get well. (KATHERINE *half-frowns, half-smiles at this idea*) I know it's ridiulous. But what else is there? And when there is nothing else, there's got to be something.

KATHERINE Yes, of course.

JOHN (*After a moment—the final horror*) When a person has been more or less continuously insane for five years . . .

KATHERINE Yes?

JOHN There can be an annulment.

KATHERINE I didn't know that.

JOHN Neither did I. My wife found this out . . . in one of her sane periods.

KATHERINE I see.

JOHN Every time I've come up here the last months when she's been halfway . . . right, she's said she would manage, in some way she would manage to kill herself if I didn't get an annulment . . . that she is ruining my life . . . How can I make her see that now she is my life? She is the condition of my life. How can I make her see that the more I tried to destroy the meaning of marriage, the closer I came to its true meaning? . . . Maybe it's guilt that binds me. I think it's love.

KATHERINE She might improve, get well, if . . .

JOHN Could you do it?

KATHERINE An annulment?

JOHN Yes.

KATHERINE No. I guess not.

JOHN Well I did. I did it . . . I took it to her yesterday.

KATHERINE Did she understand it?

JOHN When I gave it to her, she was calm and smiling. I kneeled down beside her and said, "Here it is. It's what you wanted. But as far as I'm concerned, I'm still married to

you. I couldn't live without you." . . . She said, "No, Jack.
No. Don't say that. No." . . . I start to argue, to explain.
You start, you know, and you think they're talking perfect
sense, and then you know they're not. I never know when
I go to see her if she's going to spit at me, or hold out her
arms and say, "Here's my boy." And I don't know which is
real . . . Anyway, now it's done . . . How can you annul
your life?

KATHERINE   It's just a word.

JOHN   I've tried to get through to her to talk to her about the
letter, but each time she clouds over. She slips away into
another time. "Darling, you talked in your sleep last night,
but I didn't have the heart to slap you." . . . Then some days
she sleeps for hours and hours and they get afraid and slap
her awake, gently, but they slap her and ask, "Who are you?
What's your name?" And she looks around like a startled
child and says, "Jennifer Sparrow" . . . and when they smile
approval, she smiles back and goes to sleep again . . . Who
are you? . . . Who are you? . . . I wake up some nights, bolt
upright, and I think they're slapping me, and I find myself
calling out . . . "John Sparrow. I'm John Sparrow."

KATHERINE   You must have loved her very much.

JOHN   Yes, and also hated her very much too, I imagine. Or
why did I . . . Husbands and wives shouldn't be allowed to
testify in or out of court as to the nature of their marriage.
What they give is not truth, but guilt or shame or remorse,
or memories tempered to what they can live with . . . "Who
are you sleeping with, Jack?" she asks. I try not to answer,
but she knows. She knows me. She loved it in me, the reaching out, the need to be part of a woman's life.

KATHERINE   And what do you tell her?

JOHN No one I can care for . . . And she cries. (*There is a long moment of silence. He has told the story again, and he hates himself for having told it, but he knows he had to tell it. Finally*—) Well, the sun's somewhere over there . . . We got through the night without incident . . . Congratulations.

KATHERINE (*Weakly*) Congratulations.

JOHN Who cried "Help" anyway? . . . I'm sorry for my long and boring story.

KATHERINE (*Flatly*) I'm sorry for mine.

JOHN Now you can see why I haven't told that story for two years . . . Merry Christmas.

KATHERINE Yes. Merry Christmas.
  (JOHN *moves toward his door. As he passes her, she turns and looks at him. He stops. They look at each other for a moment, and then she touches his cheek with her hand*)

JOHN Please . . . I'm sick of pity.

KATHERINE Why do you have to give it a name? I want to hold you. I want you to hold me. (*They are suddenly in each other's arms, kissing desperately, and holding each other with gratitude. He kisses her hair, her eyes, and suddenly she starts to cry, and she goes out of control. She turns from him to hide her tears, and she goes to her bed and sits, turned away from him. He looks down at her for a moment. He leans over and strokes her hair, comforting her. He holds her head against his thigh. The passion is suddenly gone. Through her subsiding tears*) I'm sorry. I'll be all right in a minute. (*He crouches beside her, and puts his arms around her, comforting her gently*) It's not easy . . . I've never been with . . .

63

JOHN (*Very quietly*) I'll go now.

KATHERINE (*With a little move, she stops him from going*)
I'll be all right. Just hold me a minute. I'll be all right.
    JOHN *holds her quietly, wondering, waiting. A shudder
    as her crying finally stops, and she looks at him again*)
Thank you.
    (*A look of infinite pity comes into her face, and she
    reaches toward his face with her hand, as though to
    bestow a mercy*)

JOHN   I don't want your pity.

KATHERINE   I want yours.
    (*Overwhelmed by the simple honesty of this, he takes
    her in his arms*)

Curtain

64

Scene Two

As the curtain rises, MAE *is carrying in a tray with breakfast. The curtains are drawn back. It is about half-past nine in the morning.*

Throughout, MAE *is not surprised at anything. She takes everything in her stride, and is perhaps a little pleased at the turn in events.*

She puts the tray down, picks up the glasses from night before, and puts them on the tray with the ice bucket.

She folds up the extra blanket and puts it over couch.

KATHERINE'S *suitcase is packed and open on the couch.*

In a moment, KATHERINE *comes in from the bathroom. She is wearing a skirt, and is buttoning her blouse.*

KATHERINE Good morning, Mae.

MAE Good morning. Merry Christmas.

KATHERINE Merry Christmas. You *are* working around the clock, aren't you?

MAE I'll get my rest tomorrow when everyone else is working. I love it that way.

KATHERINE Makes you feel quite wicked, doesn't it?

MAE Absolutely sinful.

KATHERINE It's a lovely morning, isn't it?

MAE Nippy.

KATHERINE A real old-fashioned Christmas.

MAE (*Poking around the tray*)   I spared you the morning papers. It's filled with the usual, murders, robberies and disasters.

KATHERINE   Thank you.

MAE   They said downstairs you'd be leaving this morning.

KATHERINE (*Looks for a moment at* JOHN's *door, which is closed*) Yes.

MAE   That's too bad. (*Still busying herself around the room*) Did you enjoy the movies?

KATHERINE   Yes. Very much.

MAE (*Noticing the wrappings on the Christmas presents, as she empties an ash tray*)   The stores do beautiful wrappings these days, don't they?

KATHERINE (*Modestly proud*)   I did those myself.

MAE   Did you? Must have taken you hours. Mr. Sparrow's having God's own time in there trying to tie bows on his presents. Cutting the ribbons with old razor blades, too.
    (MAE *shudders.* KATHERINE *looks in the direction of the door*)
I'm afraid his poor wife won't know the difference. It's a shame, isn't it?

KATHERINE   Yes.

MAE   Every time he comes here, I always wish there was something I could do. But . . .
    (*She shrugs*)

KATHERINE   I'm sure he appreciates it.

MAE (*On her way out*)   Well, if there's anything you want . . .

KATHERINE (*Slips a bill into* MAE's *apron pocket*) If I don't see you again, thank you. You've made me feel very much at home.

MAE Thank you. It's been nice talking with you. I hope you have a very happy New Year . . . and keep well.

KATHERINE Thank you. (MAE *goes out, closing the door behind her.* KATHERINE *waits for a moment, takes a sip of coffee, then goes to* JOHN's *door and listens for a moment. She tries to open the door, but it is bolted. She knocks, tentatively, but gets no answer. She moves away, puzzled. In a moment, the door is opened,* JOHN *stands in the doorway, with Christmas paper in his hands. They look at each other for a moment, uncertain*) Good morning.

JOHN Good morning.

KATHERINE Mae said you were wrapping Christmas presents.

JOHN (*Glad that intimate talk is avoided for the moment*) Yes. I'm terrible at it.

KATHERINE Maybe I could help you.

JOHN Would you? (*He brings in the paper, ribbons and a box with small presents in it and sets them on the stool.* KATHERINE *watches him carefully during all this. Is it to be just casual talk this morning?*) I'm all thumbs when it comes to this kind of thing. I've already cut myself once. (*He looks at his finger as he holds it out, then looks up at her. She has not looked at the finger, but has continued to look at him. They look at each other a moment, and then gently hold each other. There is sadness in this holding, yet a desire to be close, to say the things that will be said*)

KATHERINE When I went to sleep . . . you left.

JOHN Yes.

KATHERINE When I woke up, I went to your door. You'd bolted it. (JOHN *shakes his head "Yes." He would rather not have to delve into all this, but it is inevitable, and he is awkward, yet loving, and not wanting to hurt*) I thought I would wake up so full of remorse and guilt. I woke up as easily as I went to sleep . . . And you'd gone. (*She looks at him and sees his inability to say anything*) I'm sorry. Should I not say—

JOHN (*Holding her, sorry to have stopped her lyrical outburst*) Yes . . . Yes. Go on.

KATHERINE Do I look very much like your wife?

JOHN (*Knows what's coming*) Not very much. No. A little. Yes.

KATHERINE You didn't really want to be with me last night, did you?

JOHN How can you say that?

KATHERINE You were being compassionate, and then suddenly I was your wife. (*He holds her, wishing to soften the pain that he may have given her*) I suppose I should have been hurt when you called me by her name . . .

JOHN I don't know why I did that.

KATHERINE I do. For the first time in two years you were sleeping with someone you could care for. You were sleeping with your wife. And I was honored . . . and suddenly it became quite simple and beautiful.

JOHN (*He looks at her, moved by what she's said*) God, you're sweet.

KATHERINE I wish you'd stayed. Did you think that by getting up and going . . . did you think by doing that you could somehow turn me into a whore?

68

JOHN   Don't say that.

KATHERINE   Such a terrible instinct to destroy it.

JOHN   Yes, I know.

KATHERINE   How I envy your wife to have been loved so much . . .

JOHN   (*Moved by her sweetness*)   There are so many things I'd like to say to you.

KATHERINE   Say them.

JOHN   (*Looks at her, wanting to say them, but the words won't come*)   I can't.

KATHERINE   It's all right.

JOHN   No, it isn't. A woman likes to hear the words, and I like to say them. Not to say them somehow leaves everything incomplete . . . But I've spoiled them for myself. It's the only honesty I have left. Not to call things by the wrong names . . . I would like to say how wonderful it would be to be married to you. But then I know I don't mean that. I have a wife I love as a wife.

KATHERINE   But you must let someone love you. And don't be ashamed of letting her love you for the hurt you've suffered . . .

JOHN   And the hurt I've given?

KATHERINE   Yes. None of us goes far without hurting. Teach us to forgive ourselves . . .

JOHN   I'm not free to love that way. I don't want to be free to love that way. It's better to say "Never" than to play around the fringes of caring. (KATHERINE *looks at him. It seems such a waste. He reaches out and touches her hand*)

69

It's so hard for us to understand the terms on which other people settle their lives. (*They look at each other a moment, and then he breaks it by reaching into the box and pulling out a particularly ghastly attempt at a bow*) I've been trying to follow instructions on how to make a fancy bow. The directions say a ten-year-old can do it. I can't.

KATHERINE (*Kneels on the floor and starts to tie a bow on a small present*) When do you go to the hospital?

JOHN In a little while, I guess.

KATHERINE There was no call, was there?

JOHN No.

KATHERINE You were afraid, weren't you, that—

JOHN Yes. I'm always afraid she might kill herself. Now with the annulment, I'm more afraid than ever. (*He goes to the window, and holds back the curtains for a moment*) I remember how many times she begged me to do something she really didn't want—for my own good— But sometimes they call to say that it's a good day, and I should hurry over.

KATHERINE I can imagine those are wonderful days.

JOHN Yes. We don't realize how important it is to have someone to remember with. Without her I have no past.

KATHERINE (*Holding up the present*) How does that look?

JOHN Great . . . Very fancy. Maybe too fancy.

KATHERINE (*Not looking at him*) Yes, I see. I suppose it's impossible to keep secrecy out of adultery (*Looks up at him*) I'll never think of this as adultery.

JOHN (*Touched by everything this woman says, he smiles at her*) Thank you.

70

KATHERINE (*Stops making the bow*) No, this is too good. You'd better do the ribbons.

JOHN I'd better do it all. I'm famous for my wrappings. My presents are always good for a laugh. (*He takes a charm bracelet, and some paper and ribbons and sits with them in his hand for a moment*) How easily we talk about death and suicide when we're young. My wife and I made a pact, "If ever I get an incurable disease, kill me and make it look like suicide." . . . It's a way of making love, isn't it? In the health and vigor of youth, I put my life in your hands. That's how much I love you. My wife always used to say, "I want to die first. I couldn't live without you." She said it a lot. We'd get into quite an argument as to who was going to die first. She was very sentimental. (*Toward the end of this, he has put the charm bracelet in the middle of the paper, pulled up the sides of the paper, and twisted a length of ribbon around it and knotted it*)

KATHERINE She found the right man.

JOHN I guess most people do . . . There. (*He holds up his crude wrapping.* KATHERINE *is moved, but smiles*) Is it really so ghastly?

KATHERINE No. It's just that . . . No. It's beautiful. (*She has to turn away from him*)

JOHN After all, it's the spirit of the thing, not the wrapping.

KATHERINE Yes.

JOHN If you ever get a present without a card and wrapped like this, you'll know who sent it.

KATHERINE (*Looks at him seriously*) Yes. I'll know.

JOHN Have you heard from your boy?

KATHERINE   The Infirmary called to say they had released him, and he had gone to his room to pack.

JOHN   Did your husband try to call again?

KATHERINE   Yes, this morning. But there was a mix-up. The call wasn't completed. (*As though in answer to his unasked question*) I'm going to him. To London.

JOHN   That's good.

KATHERINE   Yes.

JOHN   The beautiful complexity.

KATHERINE   (*Not looking at him*) I'd always thought of adultery as shared ecstasy . . . shared excitement . . . I'd never realized it could be shared sadness . . .

JOHN   Yes.

KATHERINE   What will you do tonight?

JOHN   I don't know. Probably go to the movies. (*They look at each other as time runs out*)

KATHERINE   When my son comes . . .

JOHN   Yes, I know. I'd like to write.

KATHERINE   No.

JOHN   I was going to send you a copy of my book.

KATHERINE   I wonder if I have to read it now. I'll find a copy. *The Comfort of Your Company.*

JOHN   Yes.

KATHERINE   Maybe someday . . . maybe we could be friends.

JOHN   I'm no good as a friend.

KATHERINE   That's sad.

JOHN Yes.

KATHERINE What's going to happen to you?

JOHN I'm fine.

KATHERINE Yes, of course. We're all fine . . . I don't want to say "Good-bye."

JOHN It's impossible, isn't it?

KATHERINE You knew it would be.

JOHN Yes.

KATHERINE I'll know next time . . . Just let me say "I love you." (*Shakes his head*) Don't be angry. I do. This moment I do . . . I don't care about what's going to come . . . but I couldn't leave with that all choked up in me . . . (*The phone rings*) This will be London. (*She hesitates for a moment, then goes to the phone and picks it up. JOHN makes a gesture—Does she want him to get out? She shakes her head "No."*) Hello . . . Oh, yes. Thank you. (*She hangs up*) My son is on his way up. (*Smiles*) I knew it would be like this.

JOHN (*Approaching her*) I would like to give you something . . . something silly to . . .

KATHERINE I'll remember.

JOHN I have nothing. (*All he has found in his pocket is a penny*) A penny. (*He holds it out to show her*)

KATHERINE (*Reaching for it*) I'll take that.

JOHN Give me something.

KATHERINE I have nothing either . . . (*Reaches in her pocket*) A handkerchief . . . (*She holds it out. He takes it*)

73

JERRY (*Offstage*) Hey, Mom. (*The sound of running feet outside*)

KATHERINE I'll send him on an errand or something for a moment . . . (JOHN *moving casually toward his door, shakes his head "No."* KATHERINE *continues urgently*) Yes.

JERRY (*Outside. He knocks heavily on the door*) Mom . . . it's Jerry.

KATHERINE (*Whispers*) I'll knock.
 (JOHN *stops at his door a moment, and looks at her, then exits, closing the door behind him*)

JERRY (*Outside*) Mom. (*He knocks again*)

KATHERINE (*Opens the door*) Yes, Jerry, come in.

JERRY (*A nice, open-faced boy of thirteen comes in. He is carrying a couple of wrapped gifts*) Merry Christmas, Mom. (*He gives her a bear hug and a kiss on the cheek*)

KATHERINE Merry Christmas, Jerry. How are you feeling?

JERRY Terrific. Here. (*He holds out a flower box for her*)

KATHERINE (*Taking it*) What's this?

JERRY I know you don't like that kind very much, but it's all I could get.

KATHERINE (*Opening the box*) What is it?

JERRY You'll see.

KATHERINE (*She takes out a single gardenia corsage* Oh, it's lovely, Jerry. Thank you. (*She kisses him on the cheek*)

JERRY Is it okay?

KATHERINE You know it is.

JERRY Here's something else. (*He shoves a small box at her*)

74

KATHERINE Goodness. What is it?

JERRY Whatever it is, it's mighty small.

KATHERINE (*Unwrapping present*) Good things come in small packages. (*She has unwrapped a small bottle of perfume*) Oh, how nice.

JERRY That's your kind of perfume, isn't it?

KATHERINE It sure is. You're very observant. How did you get it in the Infirmary?

JERRY A fellow got it for me. I got something for Dad too. It's in my suitcase downstairs. Hey, we gotta go.

KATHERINE This is wonderful, Jerry. Thank you.

JERRY I'm sorry it's so small, but holy cat, that stuff's expensive.

KATHERINE A little goes a long way. I won't open it now. I'll keep it for London.

JERRY Okay.

KATHERINE I'd better finish dressing. I'm all packed except a few things.

JERRY (*Noticing* JOHN's *things on the dresser*) What's this stuff?

KATHERINE Oh . . . don't go peeking. I mean . . .

JERRY (*Teasing*) What is it?

KATHERINE (*Herding him away*) Now come on, play fair . . . Over there's a present for you. Open that. (JERRY *makes a beeline for the presents. The phone rings.* KATHERINE *picks it up*) Hello. Yes, this is Mrs. Johnson. I'll hold on. (*To* JERRY) It's London. (*Then, into the phone*) Yes, Dick . . .

Hello . . . Yes, I know you have. (*A long pause, after which she interrupts him to let him know she can't talk. He has obviously said that he has been trying to reach her*) Yes, but . . . Jerry's here. Yes . . . He looks fine.

JERRY (*He has opened his present, and loves it. It is a camera*) Hey, Mom. (*He rushes over and throws his arms around his mother and kisses her*) Thanks, Mom. Gee, that's great.

KATHERINE (*Into the phone*)   That's Jerry being grateful.

JERRY (*Into the phone* KATHERINE *is still holding*) Hi, Dad . . . Be right there. Hey, Merry Christmas. (*Takes the phone*) I got a crazy present for you . . . What? . . . Oh, I'm fine. (*He hands the phone back to his mother, and studies his camera*)

KATHERINE (*At the phone*) He looks a little pale, but they say it's all right for him to come . . . We're both coming. (*She listens a moment to his reaction of pleasure, and smiles*) We're practically out the door . . . Yes, it will be good to see you too.

JERRY (*Impulsively taking the phone from* KATHERINE)   Hey, Dad, I've grown a whole inch. And I've put a half-inch on my muscle . . . the right arm . . . Okay. (*He hands the phone back*)

KATHERINE (*Into the phone*) What are those beeps? . . . Oh, well we'd better save the money. The plumber finally came . . . No, I won't tell you how much it cost. I don't want to spoil your Christmas . . . Yes, I forgot too. Merry Christmas . . . It's a nice day here too, so everything should be all right . . . Here he is. (*To* JERRY) He wants to say something to you. (*Into the phone*) Tomorrow then. (*She gives the phone to* JERRY *and goes on packing*)

Peter De Visé and Barbara Bel Geddes, as JERRY and KATHERINE

JERRY (*Into the phone*) Yes, Dad . . . Yeah. I'll take care of her . . . Right . . . Right . . . She looks fine . . . Right. Okay, Dad . . . See you tomorrow . . . Oh, Dad, I got a new girl . . . I'll tell you about her. I got her picture. Give you something to live for . . . 'Bye. (*He hangs up*) Gosh, you can hear just as clear . . .

KATHERINE Darling, tuck this robe in the top and close it up while I finish.
   (*She goes into the bathroom to get her compact*)

JERRY (*Packing*) You got more tissue paper than clothes in here . . . Where's the rest of your stuff?

KATHERINE At the station in Boston.

JERRY Did you say close it up?

KATHERINE Yes, and you can take it downstairs. I'll meet you. Get a cab.

JERRY I told them to have one waiting. (*Looks out the window*) It's there.

KATHERINE I'll just be another minute . . . so you go ahead.

JERRY Dad told me not to let you out of my sight. I'm responsible, he says.

KATHERINE Well, you be responsible downstairs.

JERRY That's your old trick . . . "I'm ready," you say, and a half-hour later you appear. (*He gets her coats*) How many coats you got?

KATHERINE You never know what kind of weather we're going to run into. Daddy says it's spring in London.

JERRY I got one coat, period.

77

KATHERINE (*Coming back in*) With a woman it's different. You take two coats and I'll take two . . . and run along.

JERRY We got about three minutes, Mom.

KATHERINE Jerry, come on. Do what I tell you to do. Run along with the bag. I'll be right there. See, I'm all ready.

JERRY Then why don't you come along now?

KATHERINE (*Not too sternly. A little smile*) Jerry, vamoose.

JERRY Dad said . . .

KATHERINE Mother says.

JERRY (*Takes the suitcase and starts to go*) Okay, but if you're not down in thirty seconds, there's going to be hell to pay, mother or no mother. (*As he goes, he starts counting*) One and two and three and . . .

(KATHERINE *is alone for a moment. She picks up pocketbook, and moves toward* JOHN's *room. She opens the door to go in when the phone in his room rings. She turns back into her room, afraid, wondering, listening*)

JOHN (*In his room*) Yes? . . . Hello, Doctor . . . Oh, that's great. I'll be right over . . . I understand, but a day's a day, isn't it? . . . Tell her, I'll— What? . . . Hello, Jennifer . . . How are you? . . . Yes, it's Christmas. Merry Christmas to you . . . (KATHERINE *turns toward the door to the hall, and waits there a moment. She is smiling and she is crying*) I got a whole raft of presents for you . . . Yes, my crazy wrapping. Wait till you see . . . Ghastly . . . This is wonderful, Jennifer . . . My God, it's so wonderful.

(KATHERINE *goes into the hall, and*

The Curtain Is Down)